A TALE OF SURVIVAL, TRANSFORMATIONS AND WISDOM

The Life of Ruby Walters

SALLY JASPERSON

To order additional copies of this book, contact:
Xlibris
844-714-8691
www.Xlibris.com
Orders@Xlibris.com

ISBN:	Softcover	978-1-6641-9821-0
	Hardcover	978-1-6641-9822-7
	EBook	978-1-6641-9820-3

Print information available on the last page

Rev. date: 11/04/2021

CONTENTS

PROLOGUE

Krissy Jo Lee Jasperson, my daughter-in-law, has this advice framed and mounted on the wall above her dresser.

KRISSY

May your name bring courage of the pioneer;
The desire to try what's new;
Time to listen and to hear the small voice inside of you;
Patience with what seems unclear;
The will to strive anew;
Perception to see through mere pretense to the tried and true;
Strength to sustain those who fear;
The sad and the lonely, too;
Laughter that will spread good cheer through the gray skies
and the blue.
Your name is blessed, Krissy, dear, with that wisdom
given to few.

With love from your great great aunt Ruby
3:30 a.m., June 30, 1979

I wonder. What kind of woman would write such a message to a just-born great grandniece at 3:30 in the morning—and place this kind of responsibility on her?

Who was this great great aunt who wanted this baby to be named Krissy?

I learned that Ruby was sixty-seven years old when she wrote this message. That same night she also wrote a short history of her mother Georgie and her Aunt Chrissie, the Mahoney sisters who grew up on a ranch in the high desert country of southwestern Idaho. She wanted Krissy to inherit the qualities she loved about her Aunt Chrissie. For some reason, skipping several generations, she chose Krissy.

I talked to Krissy's grandmother Rae Marrs, daughter of Ruby's younger brother Irving. I learned that Ruby, though she experienced some good times, also lived through many harsh, abusive experiences. The fact that she survived amazed me. And somehow, after each abuse, instead of caving in, she just seemed to move on.

CHAPTER 1.

HEAVEN ON EARTH

Aunt Chrissie was born in 1890 in Weiser, a settlement in southwestern Idaho Territory. Her younger sister Georgie, Ruby's mother, was born in 1892, also in Weiser, after Idaho became a state. They were the only children of George and Hattie Mahoney. Chrissie married Frederick Walters in 1906, and Georgie married his brother Charles in 1910. (Frederick and Charles were two of six children. Charles was the youngest. Their mother Martha died shortly after he was born. Their father, William Henry Walters, rather than turning them over to relatives, kept all six children. He instilled in each of them a feeling of self-worth.) The brothers lived on cattle ranches next to each other outside the mile-high village of Three Creek (now a ghost town), a few miles north of the Idaho border with Nevada. They started rearing families. Georgie and Charles had three children: Ruby, Bill and Irving. Chrissie and Fred had four children: Milas, Pearl, Ella and Rema. Their eldest daughter, Pearl, was just two years older than Ruby. The double-cousins became inseparable. They lived interchangeably in each other's houses. Georgie would sometimes take Ruby's two younger brothers with her when she went away and leave Ruby with Pearl and Chrissie on the adjoining ranch, which was named Heaven on Earth. Ruby didn't mind being left there. For her it was truly heaven on Earth.

Sixty years later, on that night Krissy was born, Ruby wrote a personal memoir, "What is Heaven on Earth?" It describes the simple pleasures of that happy place—what it was like for her as a child of seven in 1919.

What Is Heaven on Earth?

Heaven on Earth is the smell of warm fresh milk as the tiny streams from each teat splash into the bucket held firmly between your knees while the kittens, sitting up on their hind legs in a semicircle five or six feet beyond the cow's tail, wait to be squirted with a strong jet of delicious warm milk which they lick hungrily from their fur—an aroma to be recalled and re-smelled all of your life.

The tangy, grassy smell of warm urine as it splashes into the dust between your horse's spraddled legs is another aromatic gift from the gods of nature which you can keep forever and forever.

Holding in your arms the warmth and softness that is a tiny puppy, too young to open its eyes, is a delight you can never, ever forget. The daily trip to visit the puppies, hidden away under the back steps, is a quiet thrill. Looking under their stubby tails to see how many males and how many females makes you feel very knowledgeable and grown-up.

To sit in the dark and stroke a sleeping cat until tiny sparks shoot from its soft fur is communion with Life.

Uncle Fred always "gave" each child a horse. Then, as the "owners" outgrew that horse, or moved away from the ranch, he "gave" the same horse to the next child. My horse's name was Keno, and during the time that I "owned" him, my beloved cousin,

Pearl, also owned a gray saddlehorse whose name was Sailor. We were told that Uncle Fred had bought Sailor from a circus so, of course, we immediately began to teach him tricks. He was a wonderful student and learned fast. Soon he would come to us from wherever he was whenever we called his name and motioned.

"Owning" a horse meant sharing the delightful responsibility of the weekly trip to the post office and store (both in the same little rock building). For this, we were allowed to use saddles because it was too far to ride bareback, perhaps three or four miles each way. It was an important duty; the mail orders were going out to Sears and Roebuck and to Montgomery Ward. Then, too, Aunt Chrissie somehow found time for quite a lot of letter-writing. And who could know what we might bring back? Sometimes there were letters for the various hired men, or for Aunt Chrissie, or business letters for Uncle Fred, or—best of all—there might be a mysterious package, which really was mysterious.

Now, almost sixty years later, I remember those tranquil rides down the lane beside the little creek bordered by willows where Grandpa Mahoney lived in his pretty little frame cabin, up the slope to the level flatland that stretched all the way to the valley where the store-post office huddled up close to the dry, rocky hill behind it. We never hurried on those trips, riding along side by side, talking, dreaming—talking was the beauty of companionship in slow motion.

And I remember the chicken hawks. Long before we'd be aware of any unseen danger from the skies, the chickens would begin to run for a hiding place; mother hens would start to cluck frantically to those little bits of yellow fluff to hurry up and hide under their outspread wings. But often as not, the hawk swooped down and snatched up a tiny straggler.

Then there was Sweetie. This chicken had various names, but I called her "Sweetie" because she would always sing when we played a certain record on the Victrola. She didn't get to sing very much, though, because Uncle Fred had forbidden us to play that *record. I never did know why it was taboo. The only line I remember now was, "If I can't get the sweetie I want, I pity the sweetie I get." ***

The real center of activities at the ranch was not the hayfields, not the blacksmith shop nor even the corrals. It was the long kitchen table where fifteen hard-working men and five or six children could eat at the same time. Aunt Chrissie or our hired girl would work the huge pans of dough on that table. There, too, they paddled the butter, a miracle to behold. The thick, rich cream was poured into the churn, and somebody— frequently one of us kids—then turned the handle until little globs of butter began to form. Then one of the women, who had been keeping an eye on our progress, would decide that it was time to work the butter. She would remove the beater and pat the little globules together into one big cream-colored ball which she placed in a bowl, covered with a snowy cloth and, surely, feeling a sense of proud accomplishment, took it to the cupboard down in the spring-house…

We knew that sheepmen were scum, and that ranchers had shot many of them because sheepherders would cut your fences and let their animals devour your grass. They were also unwelcome on the free range because, wherever they went, they destroyed the land by eating the grass, roots and all. It would take years for the grass to return.

Ruby also mentioned that she was dimly aware of feuding among the cattlemen themselves.

*Recorded by Paul Whiteman in 1923. The bouncy tune was composed by Jean Schwartz and written by Joe Young and Sam M. Lewis (Victor #19139).

The difficulties, I suppose, were mostly over water. Good grazing land was certainly important and well worth fighting over, but cattlemen could not survive unless they owned land near a creek that would produce hay for winter feeding.

She went on to tell how water was precious in the house, too.

It had to be brought up from the springhouse by the bucketful—each bucketful weighing a ton by the time you'd made your third trip… To this day, I don't take a bath more than once or twice a week, and even then, reluctantly!

Yes, that was Heaven on Earth, though I did not stay at the ranch all the time. Every now and then Georgie, our mother, would feel a maternal spasm and would pick me up and take me to wherever she and the two little boys happened to be living at the moment.

I don't know how to describe Georgie. She loved life, people and animals, and I have never heard anyone say an unkind word about her. She was charming, gifted and witty. It was, however, a mistake for her to become a mother. She should never have had children. I say that, not because she didn't seem to love us when she was with us, but rather because she could not accept responsibility for our welfare. Without warning, she would leave us unattended with little or no food in the house. I can remember standing on a wooden box, pouring cornmeal into a pan of water on the stove in an attempt to make mush for Irving, who couldn't have been more than two or three years old at the time.

Ruby didn't resent her mother's neglect. However, she always looked forward to returning to the stability of her Aunt Chrissie's ranch.

CHAPTER 2.

WANDERINGS

Over the years Ruby wrote a detailed family history.

Unfortunately, "Heaven on Earth" didn't last. Ruby still stayed with Chrissie and Pearl most of the time, but her mother would come occasionally and take her to wherever she happened to be at the time. Georgie, becoming more and more undisciplined, no longer seemed able to manage her children or her house. She started running around with different men. Her husband Charlie still loved her but couldn't control her, so he just left.

At one point, Georgie and her children were living in Twin Falls. Georgie was spending a good deal of time with a "very handsome young fellow with pretty clothes and very shiny boots," as Ruby recalled.

And not too long after this, Georgie and the children moved to an abandoned gold-mining town, Leesburg. (The boomtown, at 6,500 feet in the Salmon Valley, was crowded with about 7,000 miners and followers in the 1860s. Now it was almost empty.) They lived with her cousin Vanta Mahoney, one of seven children born to Georgie's Uncle Elza Mahoney and his wife Alice.

Ruby continues: *The fact that he was Georgie's first cousin did not seem to dampen the ardor of their relationship. She was postmistress of Leesburg, a ghost town even at the time, where not more than a couple of dozen miners might drift into town in search of a letter during the entire month. Her job left plenty of time for lovemaking, and she made it.*

It was during this time that Ruby sometimes ended up in bed with her mother and Vanta.

"Vanta was responsible for one of the greatest physical thrills of my life."

He was stretched out on the bed between my mother and me. He had an arm around each of us and my body was pressed close to his. He was hugging both of us. I was seven or eight years old. That memory confuses me even to this day: When does the desire to be petted and loved become a sexual need?

While in Leesburg, Ruby added, she and her two brothers "*happily roamed that wild, mountainous country like little animals; a country where the trees, rivers, rocks and mountains were all gigantic, where fierce winds made the timbers groan at night and snow was sometimes higher than the top of the door.*

"*But Leesburg summers were indescribably beautiful. The sensuous pleasure of walking together, barefoot, down the dusty road beside the swift river was all that any vibrant, imaginative child could desire.*"

On just such an evening, the three of them were dawdling down the mountain trail within sight of their house when they happened to see Charlie, their father, riding toward them. Ruby's memory is spotty. She couldn't recall whether or not he greeted them. She remembered feeling joy.

This next scene she had trouble dredging up.

Vanta, my mother and I were in the kitchen; Vanta was sitting in a chair, tipped back against the wall, a rifle across his knees. I felt the tension and uneasiness. My dad then came striding down the hall to the kitchen and when he was within only a few feet of Vanta, said, "Go ahead and shoot the damn thing. It's probably loaded with peas anyway" … (Another memory lapse) … And then he rode away.

Ruby and her brothers never saw their father again.

Charlie died of tuberculosis in 1927, when Ruby was fifteen. He was all alone in a sanitarium in Deer Lodge, across the Bitterroot Range in western Montana. None of his large family bothered to visit or write—except Chrissie. She wrote shortly before he died, giving him family news that he craved.

Ruby loved this warmth and caring that Chrissie showed toward everyone in the family. It is the quality Ruby wanted to pass on to Krissy from her great, great, great aunt Chrissie on that night Krissy was born.

Ruby sketchily recalled a car trip with Vanta and her mother. They took her from Leesburg to stay with Aunt Chrissie, who had by now moved to Twin Falls, where her children could get some education. Now eight years old, Ruby had never been to school. After she arrived, Aunt Chrissie hired a private tutor so Ruby could learn to read. And as she said, "I learned to read in no time at all and could soon join my cousins in our daily walk to and from the big regular school".

Unfortunately, Ruby's attendance at the good school was short lived. The age difference between Ruby and Pearl while living on their ranches had been of no importance— "there, I had no competition for her attention"—but life in town was a different story. Pearl, far ahead of her in school, had acquired a best friend and no longer wanted to play with Ruby. This was a terrible blow. Ruby felt abandoned and hurt. In turn, she became rebellious. She latched onto an older girl who was considered very "fast," ending up one night with her, plus her seven-year-old cousin, at a revival meeting in a big tent. They met some older boys who could drive. "They brought us home from wherever we were, at what they described as 'top speed.' Aunt Chrissie was really upset by this little escapade and tried to whip me. But I wouldn't cry."

That did it. Chrissie unceremoniously packed up Ruby's few belongings and took her back to her mother, who was now living in Ontario, Oregon, and no longer with Vanta.

From here on, things just got worse. Georgie dragged Ruby and her two brothers back and forth between Ontario and Weiser, where at least once they slept on the floor of a vacant house.

They had been living for some time on the street, half starving, when someone finally reported them to the authorities. Georgie and the three children were put in custody in jail for a couple of days. The boys were taken to an orphanage in Boise. Ruby went through several foster homes, then a stint in reform school, and finally to the home of a cousin in Oklahoma, who, one can assume, probably used her as his wife. She was twelve years old. The year was 1924. At that time in rural Oklahoma there were about fifteen men to one woman.

Though Ruby never saw Georgie again, word was sent to the two boys years later by whomever she was with at the time. They'd better come at once. Georgie was very ill and would probably die soon. They went.

An alternative story: Krissy's Grandmother Rae told me she had heard a slightly different tale. It was Vanta who took Ruby from her last foster home. Rae assumed it was to his ranch in Oklahoma. Had Vanta left mining in Idaho and moved to a ranch in Oklahoma? Or was it a different cousin who took Ruby at age twelve to live with him in Oklahoma? Rae didn't know, and Ruby didn't write any more about it.

Chapter 3.

– Walter Ely, The Judge

Little is known from the time Ruby was twelve until she surfaced in the Los Angeles area in the early 1940's. How she left her cousin's ranch in Oklahoma, or what she did afterwards, is anyone's guess. But Walter Ely was in the Marine Corps from 1941 through 1944, and Ruby met the attorney at a bar in Texas during that time. They fell in love.

Walter Raleigh Ely, Jr., was born in Texas in 1913. His father was a judge, Walter Raleigh Ely, who was prominent in Texas politics and a long-time friend of Lyndon B. Johnson. In 1935 Walter Junior received his LL. B from the University of Texas School of Law. He practiced in Texas from 1935 until 1939, then became an assistant state attorney general. (According to his bios, he was divorced and had a son, a fact never mentioned in any of Ruby's writings.)

In 1941 he left at the outbreak of World War II to join the Marine Corps. He earned a Silver Star.

By 1945 he and Ruby were married and in Southern California. (What about his ex-wife and son? Had Ruby broken up the marriage, or was his marriage already over?) Lawyers from out of state who want to practice in

California must first pass the California State Bar Exam, so Ruby put him through University of Southern California Law School by waiting on tables, doing secretarial work, doing whatever came along. Though Ruby had little formal education, she was very bright and inquisitive. She always thoroughly studied anything she came across. Walter received a Master of Laws degree in 1949 from the University of Southern California Law School.

As Walter's career progressed, they enjoyed a gracious California life in Whittier, where they owned a lovely home. They had lots of friends, and there was always enough money. Krissy's grandmother Rae said that during her high school years she spent two or three months each summer with them. Ruby loved children. Unfortunately, probably because of malnutrition in her youth and a possible case of rickets, she was unable to have any of her own. She may have looked upon Rae as a substitute daughter. This was in the early 1950s, and Ruby led a good life. She had a loving husband, fine clothing, lots of jewelry, and social standing.

And Ruby was uncomfortable.

Perhaps she kept remembering what it was like to have nothing. Maybe she felt guilty about being so comfortable, now. At this point her life changed.

In the early 1960s she began working with migrants in Oregon, especially in trying to help their children. And when in 1961 President John F. Kennedy formed the Peace Corps, she joined the first group that year and went to Nicaragua.

She didn't consult Walter.

In 1964 Walter was appointed by President Johnson to a lifetime judgeship with the U.S. Court of Appeals for the Ninth Circuit in San Francisco (the six western states). He was based in Los Angeles. (I've included a photo from the Los Angeles Times Photographic Archives showing Walter's father and son helping him put on his judicial robes for the occasion.)

But Ruby—who had returned home from her first Peace Corps assignment—again volunteered for the Peace Corps, this time to Honduras. Had she already left by the time Walter was appointed? There is no mention of her in the announcement.

CHAPTER 4.

HONDURAS

In "Up the Eagle", Ruby's story of her time in Honduras, she calls herself Opal, and keeps asking herself over and over again how, when she was in the Peace Corps, she could have been so naïve, so dumb, as to think the U.S. was helping these countries in Central America? Couldn't she see how the U.S. was just exploiting the people, how they remained poor while it took all the profits?

How long Ruby was in Honduras for this second assignment of the Peace Corps, I'm not sure. She probably returned home in 1966, at the end of the assignment. In 1969 her passport (unused) still read Ruby Ely. By 1971 her passport (this one used) read Ruby Walters.

Back in the United States, Ruby divorced Walter. Rae says she still saw him off and on, but she had started seeing other men. She evidently had a passionate, brief, love affair with a black professor at the University of California in Berkeley. Walter still loved her, though, and didn't understand why she stopped loving him. One time, years later, when Rae was with him at some function with a group of dignitaries, he took her aside and asked, "Rae, do you know why she stopped loving me?"

At some point, however, Walter did marry another woman.

Sometime during the 1970's Ruby refused to pay income tax to a nation that supported the Vietnam War. She returned to Honduras to apologize to her friends. By this time, she was vehement about her dislike of capitalist countries that supported dictators who kept their people in poverty so that they—and the United States—could rake in the profits. She also defied U.S. travel restrictions and visited Cuba. She was impressed with how happy and healthy everyone there seemed. Fidel Castro's revolution made complete sense to her. She wanted the same for Honduras.

In Honduras she lived in Tegucigalpa, the capital, with a group of people who thought as she did. In some danger of being discovered, they were never sure if there was a spy among them. But they didn't let that bother them much, she said. They were intent on creating their revolution. Ruby said she even started running guns at one point. She felt loved in this place, and the woman who worked for her—Lela Panamena—loved her unconditionally. But then Ruby would sigh and say, "But she loves anything to do with the U.S."

In 1973 Ruby was shot in the face, possibly by an eleven-year-old boy she had upbraided for petty thefts, though it could have been by a government spy or someone paid by the CIA. One eye was shot out of its socket, bones in her face were broken, and she lost most of her teeth.

In "Up the Eagle," she writes:

I awakened with the feeling that my head was wet. Everything else seemed normal. It was pitch dark and the katydids were still bursting their fat bellies with that shrill, deafening clamor.……I wondered if I had heard someone scratching around in the dresser drawers. If so, could it have been Adolfo looking for my billfold? Dear, stubborn, proud little Adolfo would steal anything, but his possessive love and thin, starved body had stood between me and utter loneliness for these many months.

I felt my head. It really was wet. I reached out and found the flashlight on the bedside table, switched it on and looked at the clock. Exactly two o'clock. I got up and lit the kerosene lamp on its little corner shelf above the bed. Then I saw my nightgown. The heavy lace yoke was soaked with blood, and a large pool of blood was seeping into the pillow where my head had lain. The door to the living room, which I always closed just before going to bed, was open. My hands were smeared with fresh blood. I felt no pain but knew I was hurt.

Flashlight in hand, I walked across the bedroom and living room to the front door where I paused for a second, listening to the frantic katydids. Then I unlocked the door, crossed the adobe porch and dirt patio and stepped down to the porch floor. The caretaker opened the door before I could knock. His wife, all frowzy from bed, peered over his shoulder, and his two oldest daughters were standing behind him. I said nothing, just turned the flashlight on my face. He looked stunned. "My God! Someone has hurt Dona Opal." Still without a word, I turned around and went back to my bedroom and sat on the edge of my bed. Blood dripped from my head to the floor and I was thankful for the red tile, exactly the color of blood.

Drip. Drip. Drip. I sat there thinking about Adolfo, hoping he hadn't done this. But he probably had. No one knew more about the house than he. He even knew how to crawl into the attic from outside. Then, too, he knew where I kept my machete which he had bought for me. But even if he had done this, it was my fault. I should have been more patient. Our final showdown about stealing, just a week ago, could have been avoided. He looked so hurt when I'd told him to get the hell out and never come back. He had started to apologize again but I wouldn't listen, and his soft brown eyes had filled with tears as he turned and started down the dusty road toward the gate. I had hated seeing him go because teaching him and the caretaker's oldest boy—both of them eleven—to read and write had been the only worthwhile thing I had done during these long months of waiting for my part in the action.

No one was quite sure who shot Ruby. The doctors didn't expect her to live. She was placed in a local hospital, with Lela never leaving her side, though she had eight children of her own. Miraculously, Ruby survived. She stayed in that hospital for a month, always fearing the appearance of someone she didn't know. She was never left alone.

As soon as she was able to travel, the U.S. Embassy arranged to fly her out of the country. Many of her village friends came to the airport to see her off. They included Lela, with tears in her eyes, and seven of her eight children. Before she left, a friend she didn't know quite as well took her aside and said, "Ruby, I think you should know, the CIA paid $100 to have you beaten. I used to do what you've been doing, and I still hear things."

CHAPTER 5.

NEVADA

Ruby's escape landed her in Oakland. She spent months in a medical facility in Berkeley for special eye treatments. Then Ruby contacted Rae, whom she now considered her closest family member. She asked Rae to drive to Berkeley, pick her up, and take her to her home in Reno.

Rae says Ruby's family had dwindled. Irving (Ruby's younger brother and Rae's dad) had long since gone off by himself somewhere. He was divorced from Edna (Rae's mom. Ruby never liked her too much, thought she was a lightweight). Rae was also recently divorced. She and Jackson Marrs had two teenaged daughters, Jaci (Krissy's mom) and Kerri Jo.

Ruby lived with Rae for a short time. Jaci says that the injury left Ruby's face badly scarred, though the doctors had been able to repair her damaged eye. Ruby didn't seem to let this bother her, though. At one point she was a shill (a pretend gambler) at the Mapes Hotel, but she moved on to become a secretary at the Sierra Arts Foundation in Reno. She bought a condo.

Walter, always wanting to help her, sent her money and showered her with a new car almost every year. The judge sold their home in Whittier and sent her half the money. She accepted all these things, but never went back to him.

Krissy, born in 1979, grew up in Winnemucca. Krissy says she would see Ruby in Reno when visiting grandmother Rae. She remembers always being uncomfortable around great great aunt Ruby, who kept asking her to memorize things, to keep learning new things.

One question that always puzzled Ruby was why her brother Irving, who also lived in Winnemucca, would have nothing to do with the family. Krissy's mother Jaci was his granddaughter. She lived with her husband Ron Lee and their two children Krissy and Jeremiah Lee, who were Irving's great grandchildren. Jaci says he would just never leave his ranch. Ruby then mentioned that Krissy, at eleven, was a delightful young lady.

And during all of this time, Ruby was in contact with her friends in Honduras and working on their "cause."

She also kept in touch with Lela, who wanted to come to the U.S. Ruby gave her the money to visit Reno. Lela wanted to stay. Having no husband in Honduras, she found a man who married her—Stephen Moritch—thus giving her the road to citizenship and allowing her to bring up her children in her adopted country. The arrangement worked out agreeably. Even though the family later settled in Sacramento, they always kept in touch with Ruby.

At one point, Ruby sent Rae, Lela, and a male writer back to Honduras for a visit. I asked Rae if Ruby was trying to "convert" her. Rae said, "No, but she wanted me to visit other countries, to see what other peoples' lives were like." Rae said one day Lela took them to a home where dozens of people were jammed into just a couple of rooms. The occupants slept in shifts. When one person got up to go to work, another would take his place in the bed.

In 1980, when filling out a Family Emergency Guide, Ruby entered her employer as Sierra Arts Foundation, but entered her occupation as "Revolutionary."

Walter Ely, living in Sunset Beach at the time, died in 1984. Interestingly, in his obituary, in Wikipedia, and in many other articles about him, there was no mention of Ruby or the fact that he was ever married to her.

Ruby moved in with Rae again in 1983 when her health began to deteriorate. Rae took care of her until Ruby's death. During this time there was a lot of correspondence between Ruby and her friend, Ace Hayes, a journalist with a reputation for incendiary articles. The two of them were determined to carry on the "historic struggle" against the "reality of treason, lies and ignorance."

They persevered but became more and more discouraged. In one letter Ace wrote,

"I've failed

"I've failed

"I've failed"

He sent Ruby what he called a "Skeleton Key to the Gemstone File," an outline of a huge, detailed project by an American man named Bruce Roberts, who listed treasonous actions by government officials and others, starting with Aristotle Onassis in 1932, continuing with the Mafia, Howard Hughes, the Kennedys, Nixon, Watergate, McNamara, Gerald Ford, and on. Ace ended his outline with, "Which brings us almost to the present time. Ford, Kissinger, and Rockefeller squat like toads on the corpse of America."

In 1990 Ruby died of cancer in a Reno hospital while holding Rae's hand.

GALLERY

Chrissy Mahoney
Born 1890
Weiser, Idaho Territory

Georgie Mahoney
Born 1892
Weiser, Idaho

Georgie Mahoney before her
marriage to Charles Royal Walters
November 28, 1910
In Boise, ID

Family Portrait, Twin Falls
with
Georgie behind, and
Bill, Ruby, Irving, Charles

Heaven on Earth

T Quarter-Circle Ranch
Three Creek, Idaho

Georgie behind the seven double cousins;
Milas, Pearl, Ruby, Bill, Ella, Irving, Rema

Ruby, Irving and Bill with Vanta while
Living in Leesberg, shortly before
Charlie's confrontation.

Ruby and Pearl in Twin Falls
Ruby is eleven and Pearl is thirteen

Ruby and Rae

1985

After Ruby, in poor health, moved back in with Rae

Ruby, probably in her Peace Corps days, early 1960s

Walter Ely's father, Judge Walter R. Ely, and his son, William R. Ely, help him put on his judicial robes in Los Angeles, CA, 1964.

Collection: Los Angeles Times Photographic Archives

Owning Institution: UCLA, Library Special Collections,

Charles E. Young Research Library

Source: Calisphere

Here are the other instructions Ruby wrote to
baby Krissy shortly after she was born:

Krissy

You are now and will always be
The magnet that will draw together all those who love you,
The generator that will provide the flow of continuous
vibrations of love to those within your ever-expanding group,
The current that will carry your love, and theirs,
from one to the other,
The hub whose spokes, each a sturdy bond of love, will hold all
who know you within the solid circle of your goodness.